Jack Buck

FOREVER A WINNER

www.sportspublishingllc.com

Jack Buck
FOREVER A WINNER

SENIOR MANAGING EDITORS
Joseph J. Bannon Jr. and Susan M. Moyer

ART DIRECTOR
K. Jeffrey Higgerson

INTERIOR DESIGN, PROJECT MANAGER, DUST JACKET DESIGN
Kerri Baker

COORDINATING EDITOR
Erin Linden-Levy

COPY EDITOR
Cynthia L. McNew

ISBN 1-58261-606-X

Printed in Canada

Contents

Foreword
by Tony La Russa
8

Growing Up Jack
16

G.I. Jack
24

"Buck Eyes Sports"
34

Family Man
40

All-American
64

A Civic Mind
70

From the Gridiron
80

Talkin' Baseball
88

"That's a Winner"
112

It's Been an Honor
122

"So Long for Just
a While"
134

"We are thankful to God for the bat of Musial, for the arm of Gibson, for the legs of Brock, for the power of McGwire. We are all here today to say thank you to God for Jack Buck."

— *Joe Buck*

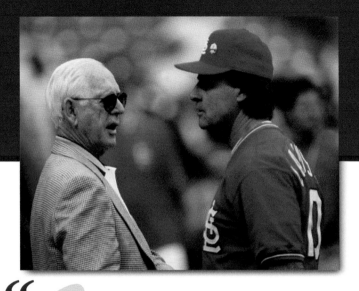

by Tony La Russa

FOREWORD

"Jack was a man of so many talents and interests—with so much knowledge. At the memorial service, I thought Dan Dierdorf's comment summed it up best. Dan said that the great majority of people knew Jack as a broadcaster. He was a Hall of Famer and he was great, but if you got to know him, his broadcasting was only one of his many talents. There was so much more to him. I thought that was a great comment, because Jack could speak on any subject and he was so interesting. He could be serious or he could be funny. I really think Jack was a genius.

The first time I met Jack was when I was back in the American League. It was a national game and I shook his hand, but that was all. Jack, of course, broadcast the '88 World Series. He's the voice on the Kirk Gibson home run, and I was in the A's dugout there in Dodger Stadium. It was heartbreaking. I didn't really get to know him until '96 when I came over to the Cardinals. From spring training on, though, I got to know him better and better, and he and Carole became very special friends of mine.

One thing he said that I'll never forget was that I had one asset I should never lose—the fact that I approach the games like a fan. Jack said the difference is that sometimes if you are in uniform, you get professional and cold and objective. You do your best, and if the other team wins, you just turn to the next page. It was always harder for me to just turn the page if the Cardinals got beat. Jack would tell me that he thought I suffered the losses and enjoyed the wins on a fan-like level and that that was a good quality and not to lose it.

The thing about Jack's style is that he was such an intelligent man and he had such wide-ranging interests that he would do an interview and it wouldn't just be cold or strictly baseball. He would introduce other pieces of life or events and draw analogies and ask questions that went way beyond just who's pitching and who's hitting. It was really fun and interesting to talk to him. If you were interviewed by him, it was a different experience. I think the fans always got a better perspective from a Jack Buck interview than from anybody else.

There is no doubt that there have been changes in the attitudes of the media and the relationships between the media and the people in uniform. It can be confrontational and it can be adversarial. Now, to a great degree the people who talk or write about the game—whatever game it is—can be personalities or stars in their own right, so there's a competition. Sometimes when they do an interview they want the public to remember how smart their questions were, as opposed to just bringing out the subject of the interview. That creates a certain pressure and some hard feelings at times. People in uniform don't trust the media like they used to. There is a lot of baiting to create controversy because they think controversy sells.

Jack started his broadcasting career before that happened, and through the years he never sank to that level. He always did a very high-class, Jack Buck-style interview. Back in the old days he was friendly with players and was respected by them and was part of the

Jack interviews San Francisco Giants manager Roger Craig. Craig and La Russa (with the Oakland A's) managed against each other in the 1989 World Series. Jack was on hand to call the series, which was interrupted by a major earthquake at Candlestick Park.

To Mom
with
Love
Rick

inner core. Even right there at the end, he was still immensely popular and trusted by the current Cardinals. Don't get me wrong, Jack could be critical during interviews, but he was always professional and honest. No one resented him for the questions he asked. Times have changed, and mostly not for the better, but Jack never changed.

When we lost Jack, we were all affected. We knew that Jack had had a very tough winter. He couldn't leave the hospital and had a series of setbacks. We also knew that his family was really suffering—any time you see a loved one go through that it is very difficult. We were used to, in spring training, having Jack come down and reconnect with the team and carry it over through the year. So when he wasn't there during spring training in 2002, that was a major adjustment and not a happy time. Everybody realized how serious his health issues were. I think we all had some very selfish moments dealing with Jack's death. We knew he was really struggling and we knew that the family had been dealing with it for so long, but we all wanted him to hang in there because we didn't want to lose him. We had the opportunity to start making adjustments to him not being there in spring training and through the first couple months of the season, but it was not something we ever came to grips with. His death was very sad.

Losing Jack and Darryl Kile so close together was incredibly difficult. We were deeply saddened by Jack's death, and deeply staggered by Darryl's death. At the time, I don't think anybody knew how the club was going to respond. We lost Darryl in the prime of his life—with a young family and everything—and people started questioning what is really important. A lot of the answers to those questions did not include going to the ballpark and playing. Nobody knew how, but we kept our thoughts and hearts together. Trying to conduct ourselves in a way that would honor and respect Jack and Darryl became important to us.

I'm sure we all wish we could have just one more day with Jack. If I could have planned our last day together, it would go something like this: Jack would have prepared something that would be meaningful and he would have written it in a way that was pure poetry, so part of that day would have been spent listening to Jack speak. My best memory of my first six years in St. Louis, on an away-from-the-ballpark basis, was going to dinner with Jack and Carole Buck. That was the best thing that happened for me and for anybody who was able to go to those dinners. I think it is important to note the partnership that Jack and Carole had. Part of the charm of those dinners was how Jack and Carole complemented each other. So, my day with Jack would start with him reading something that he wrote—which would have knocked you out because he had such a gift—and it would end with us all going to dinner. In which case, our conversation would be filled with laughter and fascination about the subjects that we would discuss.

That is how our day would go if we could just have one more day with Jack.

— Tony La Russa

Spring training was a time for Jack and the Cardinals to reconnect after a long winter apart. He was a fixture in Florida and was sorely missed when he was too sick to attend in 2002.

Jack watches batting practice with Tony La Russa at Cardinals spring training in Florida.

Growing

chapter
ONE

Jack's brother Frank (rear) was the oldest child in the family and also the wildest. He was once summoned to the principal's office to be punished, and when the principal hit him with a ruler, Frank popped him. Along came Earle Jr. (far left), and he was the opposite—a great student who never caused any problems. When Jack (far right) came along next, they kept a wary eye on him, especially the teachers. Also in the photo are Jack's mother and sister, both named Kathleen.

Up Jack

Back in Holyoke, Jack lived on Longwood Avenue in a house that was owned by his uncle and aunt, Dan and Josie Hickey. Jack's parents and their seven kids lived downstairs, while his aunt and uncle and their five children lived upstairs. It was a busy house.

Earle Buck Jr.

Earle Buck Jr., Jack's older brother, was the second oldest of Earle and Kathleen Buck's seven children. He is now retired and living in Avon Lake, Ohio.

"We were not much different than the rest of the kids in our neighborhood. We were all pretty much in the same boat.

We used to sell newspapers on the corner for about three cents apiece and made a penny a paper. When people got off the bus we'd have our papers folded, and you learned to fold a paper and hand it to a guy with your palm out to get your three cents. We hated it when someone gave us a nickel or a dime because we had to stop and make change. While you're making change people are running past you and you're not selling papers.

We were always out playing football or baseball. Recognize that times are different, things are different. We picked our own teams, set up our own fields, officiated our own games. You found out how good you were when you ended up playing right field and batting ninth. We used to settle our own arguments. There were no umpires; either you're safe or you were out. There was no arguing. That kind of carried on through most of our lives. We were used to working with people. When you want to play ball and they say "bat ninth and play right field," that's what you do. That happens in life. To get with other people and work as a team, I think that was a big priority for us.

Jack knew and I knew that he wanted to be a baseball sports announcer. We knew because we used to listen to the radio and Jack would mimic the announcers. Jack always had a keen insight into the game, even when he was a kid. One time he wrote a letter to Red

Sox manager Joe Cronin, suggesting a new lineup. To Jack's delight, Joe answered his letter, used the lineup and won the game.

When we would play pickup ball, it didn't matter which position he was playing, he kept up a running narrative of the game. One of our friends, Bill Hickey, hit the ball and while Jack was chasing the ball he'd yell, "Hickey hits a line drive," and his average and all that, to the extent that it got to be a pain in the butt and we all yelled at him to shut up.

There was a man by the name of John Curran who was the proprietor of a drug store in our neighborhood in Massachusetts, and I know a couple of times he took Jack to Fenway Park to watch the Red Sox. Jack used to tell a funny story about the first time he went to Fenway with Mr. Curran. Jack had proudly paid for his own admission to the game, but only had 75 cents left for dinner. He ordered a cheese sandwich while everyone else was feasting on steak and lobster. Jack could have died when one of Mr. Curran's friends picked up the check for everyone. He had missed the chance to eat his first steak—all he got was a lousy cheese sandwich.

We used to hitchhike down to Springfield, Massachusetts. Springfield had a team in the Eastern League at that time called the Springfield Rifles. We saw guys playing there—Mickey Vernon, who later managed Washington, and Jimmy Bloodworth, who was a second baseman, and a pitcher by the name of Alexander Carrasquel. That was a farm team of the Washington Senators. That used to be our professional sports—hitchhiking down to see the Springfield Rifles play.

Jack's father, Earle, used to commute from New Jersey on the New York–New Haven and Hartford Railroad. He was also the manager of the Erie baseball team, and when he came home, he had a ball or a bat with him. According to Jack, his father "was a great baseball player. He pitched and played first base and hurled a perfect game for Holyoke High School."

RIGHT: Jack spoke of his mother, Kathleen, as "a happy person with a hearty laugh, who loved to sing and tell jokes. She taught all the good things like honesty, respect and how to listen to your conscience." She always said, "We may not have money, but we're not poor."

After Dad passed away, we all had to dig in and work at it. My older brother Frank had already come to Cleveland, and that's one of the reasons we moved out there. I was 16 and my father died in December. I graduated the following June. The people from my father's work told me to finish high school and there'd be a job waiting for me. I got out of high school and at age 17 started work as a clerk.

Jack was working at the burger place. It meant we all had to pitch in. I can only say we made it, and I attribute that to my mother; she was a strong lady.

I think after the war when Jack went to Ohio State, he started out as a communications major or a journalism major. I told him to get out and get a degree that's going to do you something. Get a degree in accounting, where there's some jobs, and forget about this broadcasting. He did his homework, though. He used to take tape recorders to road games and watch the Columbus Redbirds play. He just persevered. He told me the story one time about when he was working at a gas station and one of his English teachers came up to him to get gas and said, "You better speak in Spanish because you're better in Spanish than you are in English."

I think the teacher felt sorry for Jack and gave him private tutoring. They got to be friends. He persevered and just got what

"Look out, here come the Buck kids!"

On the way back home from a movie, Jack (back left) and his siblings would walk through the alley and try to get into their uncle's restaurant to get something to eat. If their uncle saw them coming, though, he would close the restaurant, lock the door, and pull the shades.

One time, on the ball field, Jack (far right) was ragging a player, who threatened to throw the bat at Jack if he said another word. The kid wasn't joking. His tormentor made another comment, so he let it loose. Jack couldn't get out of the way of the bat and had to be carried home. His mother sent Jack's brother Earle (middle left, sitting next to sister Kathleen) back to get even. The kid beat Earle up. Then his mother sent Frank (middle right, holding the family dog, Snowball) after him, and the kid beat Frank up.

Who could forget

DEAR EDITOR,

How could I forget the young **Jack** Buck who sat next to me in **Miss** Forsythe's eighth-grade homeroom at Highland School. The little **poem** he wrote in my autograph book was always good for a laugh from those with whom I shared it.

*Roses are red, violets are blue
I bet there's some guy crazy
    about you
But not me!*

MARION HYNES PROKOP

he went after. He didn't lose sight of that. Regardless of what status of celebrity he might have achieved, his first love was just broadcasting ballgames. We just had a feeling that that's what he was going to do, and he did it.

When Jack got inducted in the Hall of Fame in Cooperstown in 1987, my wife and I went up there and I'm looking at the map and I see Cooperstown's pretty close to Booneville. So on the way home we stopped off in Booneville to see if we could find a history of the Bucks or any record of the Bucks.

We went to the library, and someone told us that all the village records were in Utica, New York. We were getting discouraged and started off for home when my wife said that she saw a cemetery at the end of town. We found it and I had to stop at the side of the road.

"You won't believe what I'm looking at," she told me. I looked over at the cemetery. We had parked alongside an iron fence and looking right at us were a bunch of grave markers with the name Buck on them. So we drove in and I grabbed a paper and wrote the inscriptions. One of them was Daniel Buck, who was a Revolutionary War soldier. So I got down the information and found out that he was in fact a Revolutionary War soldier. I did some research and traced the family back to Massachusetts and Francis Cooke on the Mayflower. ■

Jack almost dropped out of high school in 1941 to get a full-time job and help support his family. He would have gotten away had it not been for one teacher, Edna Kleinschmidt. She was furious when Jack told her he was leaving school. She even went to Jack's house to talk to his mother. She stomped her foot and said, **"He is not quitting school."**

Here are Jack (left), Frank (middle) and Earle as young men.

After his family moved to Cleveland, Jack honed his broadcasting skills at Indians games. He and his brother Earle would take the streetcar and sit in the bleachers. As they sat, watching the game, Jack would be calling it and Earle would yell at him to "stop" or he would move to another section of the bleachers.

Part of Jack's job after the war, while he was still in the army, was scheduling softball games, and he organized one against the 38th Triple A Battalion at Berchtesgaden. When the squad got there, there was no other team to play. The 38th didn't show, but Jack wasn't surprised. There was no 38th Triple A Battalion—he'd made up the game and gotten the rations so the team could go to Berchtesgaden and visit Hitler's former headquarters.

G.I. Jack

The War Years

In June of 1943, 19-year-old Jack Buck was drafted into the army. He first was sent to Fort Eustis, Virginia, for basic training. There he earned the rank of corporal. Jack later spent time in Georgia, California and Maryland before shipping out to Europe in February, 1945. Jack served in Eastern Europe until April, 1946. In his autobiography, That's a Winner!, *Buck recalled his experiences as a soldier, both serious, sustaining a shoulder wound, and lighthearted, playing ice hockey.*

" Beware the Ides of March. March 15 rolled around, and that was the day I was wounded. It was 5:30 in the morning. I had been made a squad leader, and I was taking out a patrol to bring back some prisoners. I knew the Germans had a particular crossroad zeroed in because of all of the shelling the day before. I talked to the squad members and told them to be quiet and not make any noise.

A group of tanks were lined up waiting to join the action. It's my guess that one of the tankers got cold and fired up his engine. As soon as I heard the engine start, I yelled. "Run!" I was scrambling for cover when an .88 hit a tree behind me and the shrapnel got me in the left arm and leg. I had a hand grenade hanging on my chest, and to this day I don't know how the shrapnel missed it. I just missed losing my left arm, not to mention having my head blown off. I was really lucky.

As I lay there, the first GI who came along took my rations. The second took my grenades. The third was a medic and he put a bandage on the wound. "Stay here," he said. "I'll send a jeep for you."

More shells started to hit, so I got up and got the hell out of there. I started walking down the road to a field hospital and lit a cigarette. One of the tankers yelled at me to put it out because it was still dark. "Screw you," I yelled back. I was angry at them because one of their tanks had started an engine, causing me to get hit.

Another of the tankers yelled, "How's your leg, soldier?" I looked down, and my pant leg was gone. I didn't even know it. Fortunately, I just had some superficial wounds on the calf of my leg. I caught up with a jeep and headed for the field hospital behind the lines.

After I came to St. Louis to work for the Cardinals in 1954, I was in the stands watching a soccer game and I recognized the goalie. I knew that I didn't know him from St. Louis, so I talked to him at halftime and we determined that after the war, we had both tried out for the 9th infantry division baseball team. His name was Frank Borghi. He got the job, and I joined the fast-pitch softball team.

In 1975, I was the emcee of a banquet at which Borghi was being honored as the goaltender for the team that beat England 1-0 in the 1950 World Cup game in Brazil. To this day, it's one of the most monumental upsets in World Cup history. We were seated at the head table, and we talked about the 9th infantry division. I asked him what regiment he was in, and he said the 47th. I said I was also. I asked him what company he was in, and he told me he was in K company. So was I. I asked what he did in K company, and he told me he was a medic. I asked how many medics there were in K company after we crossed the Remagen Bridge. He told me he was the only one, because the other medic had been wounded. We determined that he was the medic who bandaged me the morning I was hit. That's unbelievable.

▼ ▼ ▼

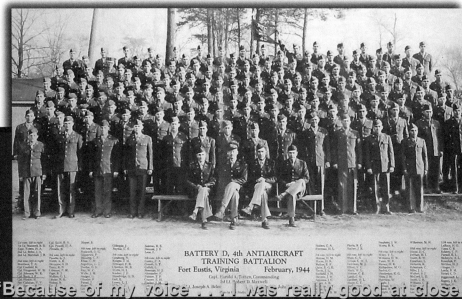

BATTERY D, 4th ANTIAIRCRAFT
TRAINING BATTALION
Fort Eustis, Virginia   February, 1944
Capt. Harold A. Totten, Commanding
1st Lt. Robert D. Maxwell

Jack's first assignment in the army was anti-aircraft training, and he was sent to Fort Eustis, Virginia, for basic training. After completing his 13 weeks, he joined the cadre as one of the instructors and was given the rank of corporal. "Because of my voice . . . I was really good at close order drill. You could hear me all over the area."

Even though I could hardly skate, I went out for the hockey team. "I'm a goaltender," I said. We had all the equipment except for the goalie, so I had a baseball catcher's chest protector and my first baseman's glove. Nobody even thought about wearing a helmet or a mask back then.

As a kid when we played hockey on the frozen ponds of Holyoke, we used a tin can for a puck. Later, when I was growing up in Cleveland, I watched the Cleveland Barons play, so I had some idea about what I was doing, but I was way out of my league. During practice a fellow skated in on me, and before I could even move my glove, he fired the puck and hit the inside of my thigh. I thought he broke my leg. My thigh read, "Spalding, Made in the USA" for about a month.

Another player fired a puck at me, and it took off before I could react. It hit my chest protector, bounced up and hit me in the Adam's apple. It knocked me back and my head hit the crossbar. They carried me off the ice. The team left for a game in Sweden without me and lost by a score of 22-1.

▲　▲　▲

One of the army's strictest rules in immediate postwar Germany was against fraternization. If the MPs caught a GI fraternizing with a German woman, he was put into

After the war, Jack's first assignment was pulling guard duty at Mooseburg, where SS troops were being held as prisoners. So many GIs had been sent home that he was pulling guard duty eight hours on, four off, 16 hours a day. According to Jack (kneeling at far right), that schedule was tough: "I had to figure a way to get out of that action. Sports was the answer."

a labor camp with no questions asked. It didn't make any difference who you were or what you had done. Those camps were awful.

That threat didn't stop some of us. Two others and I were heading back to our outfit one day when we ran into some German girls in an apartment building. We were trying to romance them, and somebody called the MPs. Here they came in a jeep. The three of us rushed to find a place to hide, and the other two were caught quickly. They couldn't find me. The MPs were ready to leave, and the Germans kept telling them, "There's one more, one more." They looked a little while longer, but still couldn't find me and finally left.

I had climbed my way to safety through a bomb hole in the roof and was lying on the roof of this three-story apartment building. Now the MPs were gone, and I came down. The Germans were still in the building, laughing about how they had the GIs arrested, and I came down the stairs and started screaming and firing a pistol into the ceiling. I scared the hell out of them, and while they were diving for cover I ran out the door. I never saw the two other guys again, but I know they ended up in a labor camp.

Jack's supervisor on the *J.H. Sheadle* was the deck watch. The two didn't get along. They got into a fight when Jack threw a pot of tea leaves into the wind just as his boss came around the cabin. The leaves smacked him in the face. Jack took off running, but he didn't get very far. Jack recalled, "It's tough to avoid a fight when you're stuck on a boat."

Army of the United States

50033

Honorable Discharge

This is to certify that

JOHN F BUCK

35067459 CORPORAL 47TH INFANTRY REGIMENT 9TH DIVISION

Army of the United States

is hereby Honorably Discharged from the military service of the United States of America.

This certificate is awarded as a testimonial of Honest and Faithful Service to this country.

Given at   SEPARATION CENTER
            CAMP ATTERBURY INDIANA

Date   11 MAY 1946

VOL 96 PAGE 157

E. W. HENRY
MAJOR AC

6-6-44

"D" Day in Europe was the sixth of June, nineteen forty-four.
It was the start of the end of World War Two,
unlike anything seen before.

Ordinary men from the forty-eight states
had trained as best they knew how.
They were tough and ready and anxious to fight.
They didn't know what we know now.

They left the coast of England,
to hit the beaches of France.
They plunged into an inferno.
The devil had started his dance.

The man-made thunder,
and a storm made of steel,
introduced them to a new level of fear.
Awe overtook them, and they shared the same thought,
"What the hell am I doing here?"

Long before they fired a shot,
every man knew his chances were slim.
Even hell was never this hot.
He said goodbye to the pal next to him.

How could one live even five minutes more?
Forward was the only command.
They were headed for Death's wide-open door.
They would die with their face in the sand.

Fate played its part and guided some of them through,
but most never saw the next day.
They lie beneath a Normandy cross.
So young and so far away.

JACK BUCK
CO. K 47th INFANTRY
REMAGEN, GERMANY
MARCH 15, 1945

Jack received a Purple Heart after he was hit with shrapnel, but maintained that it was no big deal: "In some of the movies about the war, those ceremonies are a lot more dramatic than they actually are. All I remember was sitting on my hospital bed and an officer came down the aisle and said, 'John Buck?' When I identified myself, he tossed the medal to me, then moved on to the next guy."

"*Buck Eyes*

chapter
THREE

When Jack did Ohio State basketball play-by-play the first time, his classmates were assigned to listen to his broadcast and critique it the next morning. Jack remembers that, overall, "the critiques were honest and helpful," but he also never forgot what the professor told him: "You'd better find something else to do for a living."

At the far left, Jack poses for a photo with his television colleagues, including Jonathan Winters, top right.

Sports **"**

"Hey, Jack, we've come a long way since Columbus, Ohio."

JONATHAN WINTERS

One of the most inventive and influential comedians of the past half-century, Jonathan Winters worked with Jack Buck in the early years of television, at WBNS-TV in Columbus, Ohio, in the early 1950s.

" I worked two and a half years at WBNS-TV, a CBS affiliate in Columbus, from 1950 to the winter of 1953. Then I went to New York and Jack went on to work at KMOX.

We knew each other well. He was doing sports and I guess I was doing a little bit of everything. I had a couple of shows. I knew he was well into sports then.

So much was different. The equipment alone was pretty bulky. The cameras and the tripod jobs and the boxes were the size of a small flatcar, it seemed.

Needless to say, the money was a joke compared to today's salaries. Everything has changed for sportscasters and standup people and actors. I don't know what Jack started at, but I started at 75 bucks a week, which sounds like a lot of money. But unfortunately, when you're living in a housing project like we were in Columbus and have one car and are supporting a wife and child, there wasn't a lot there.

I got up to $125 a week and I went in for a $5 raise—I think Jack went in around the same time. WBNS stood close to Ohio National Bank. I asked for a $5 raise and they said, "Oh, we just don't have it." I couldn't believe it with those credits.

"We brought you along," they said. "There was very little talent at the time. We thought you had enough talent. We think you should be grateful and satisfied that you're getting a hundred and a quarter a week."

So I left.

I asked myself if I would have stayed for $5 more. I probably would have. But I went to New York with $56.46 and never turned back.

"If I can't make it in a year," I said to myself, "I'll come back. I don't know if I'll go to Columbus but I'll go someplace."

I'd see Jack from time to time here on the coast, and I'm just sorry that I didn't get to St. Louis to see him before he passed on.

I would sit with guys like Jack—not only Jack Buck but also Jack Brickhouse with the White Sox in Chicago and Joe Nuxhall. I sat in with Jack and played Whip Willis, an old pitcher or something, and had a lot of fun. He would interview me and we were on radio, which made it even better because they couldn't see me.

As we know, Jack went on to big, big things with baseball and football and every sport there was. He was a hell of a guy, a wonderful announcer, and a good man.

Thank God his son has stepped into his shoes, which are pretty big shoes to step into. Joe Buck is doing a great job and I know Jack was very proud of Joe.

I always remember he was such a likeable guy and always had a big smile. He always had something good to say to me, in turn, I would say to him, "Hey, we've come a long way since Columbus, Ohio."

It was a great treat to have known him and to have a lot of laughs and a lot of good times. I'm really sorry he's gone. There are a lot of people all over that miss that voice and his commentary on sports. But he made a big, big mark. Not everybody can say that. I'm proud to have known him. ■

The Ohio State University

hereby confers upon

John Francis Buck

the degree of

Bachelor of Arts

together with all the rights, privileges and honors appertaining thereto in consideration of the satisfactory completion of the course prescribed in

The College of Arts and Sciences

In Testimony Whereof, the seal of the University and the signatures as authorized by the Board of Trustees are hereunto affixed.

Given at Columbus on the sixteenth day of December in the year of our Lord nineteen hundred forty-nine. ▼

W. Th. Pomerene
Chairman of the Board of Trustees

Howard L. Bevis
President of the University

Chas. S. Steel
Secretary of the Board of Trustees

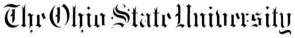
even after the family dog chewed the corner off his diploma.

With the help of the GI Bill, Jack earned his degree from The Ohio State University. His pride in his accomplishment was undiminished, even after the family dog chewed the corner off his diploma.

The scoreboard shows:

NATIONAL	1	2	3	4
ST. LOUIS	1	1	0	0
PHILADELPHIA	0	2	8	1
MILWAUKEE	0	1	0	
NEW YORK	0	1		
CINCINNATI	0	0	3	0
BROOKLYN	0	0	0	0
CHICAGO	0	1	0	0
PITTSBURGH	0	0	1	0

Jack went on the air for the first time in 1948 while he was working at the university radio station, WOSU. Not long after, he auditioned for and was offered a job with the Columbus station WCOL, where he did basketball and baseball play-by-play. He broke into television with WBNS-TV in 1952, where he worked with Jonathan Winters and hosted several sports shows.

Family

Man

chapter
FOUR

Dad once said, "Whether we're happy or sad, whether we have too much or too little, we each have to live our own life. Some never get to climb the mountain. Others soar to the top. Everyone is on their own. I've tried to teach my children what I believe. I think my kids have learned from the example I've set, and I am proud of all eight of them." Here we all are celebrating Dad's 75th birthday at Christine's house. From left to right are: Bonnie, Beverly, Joe, Dad, Christine, Jack Jr., Julie, Danny, and Betsy.

by **Julie Buck Brooks**

"As I am writing this about my dad, I am sitting at his desk in my parents' home. It is the desk he had since I was born. I see his scribbles on his desk pad; the drawers are neatly organized as they always were, just as he left it. It even smells like he's still here. It feels familiar to me in every way, and it's still really hard for me to believe he's gone.

I miss everything about him. He was my friend, my authority figure, my counselor, and my comedian. No matter the situation, he knew how to simplify it and in most cases make everything okay.

I am so grateful that I had my dad for 30 years. He was the best; he never let me down, and he always made me proud to be his daughter.

I'll always cherish the times he spent with me—Cardinals road trips, spring training, a ride in the car—it didn't matter what we did. I'll cherish every moment.

I'm especially thankful for the time he spent with my sons. "Good, fine boys," was what he used to say about them often. My married name is Brooks, and when our twins,

With Love
to My Wife Carole
and Julia --- m-
our daughter's first
day.
June 15, 1972

Jack and Matthew, were born, Dad would come to the hospital every day wearing his Brooks Brothers blazer. He'd greet the babies by opening his jacket to show them his Brooks Brothers label and call them the "Brooks Brothers." He was so thrilled with the twins. Not only did he let out a shout of joy when I told him there were two babies, he also went to more than one ultrasound appointment with us.

Just six weeks before my dad died, our third son, little Ben, was born. Even though my dad was so sick, when I told him we were going to sneak Ben into the ICU to see him, his face lit up. They did get to meet each other, and my dad reached up and grabbed Ben's little hand and smiled with tears in his eyes.

"Be smart," "Go to work, kid," "Stop calling," "Hey, you guys," . . . these are all personal memories I will always keep in my heart. For all of those who read this book, Daddy, I love you.

— *Julie*

(AKA #8, that's what he called me)

"When Jack was getting ready for a road game, he wouldn't even have time to come home and pack. Julie, Joe and I would pack a suitcase for him and meet him at Busch Stadium, with just enough time before the team left for a hug and a kiss and to hand over his bags."—Carole

"The phrase, 'random acts of kindness,' might have been invented for him. If we all do random acts of kindness, we might be able to fill the void just a bit."

— Jack Buck's daughter Christine

"We owned a racehorse named 'Almighty Buck' for a while, and Jack joked that the horse was so expensive to keep that it seemed like he was another member of the family. In his first race, Almighty Buck won at Arlington by 15 lengths."
—Carole

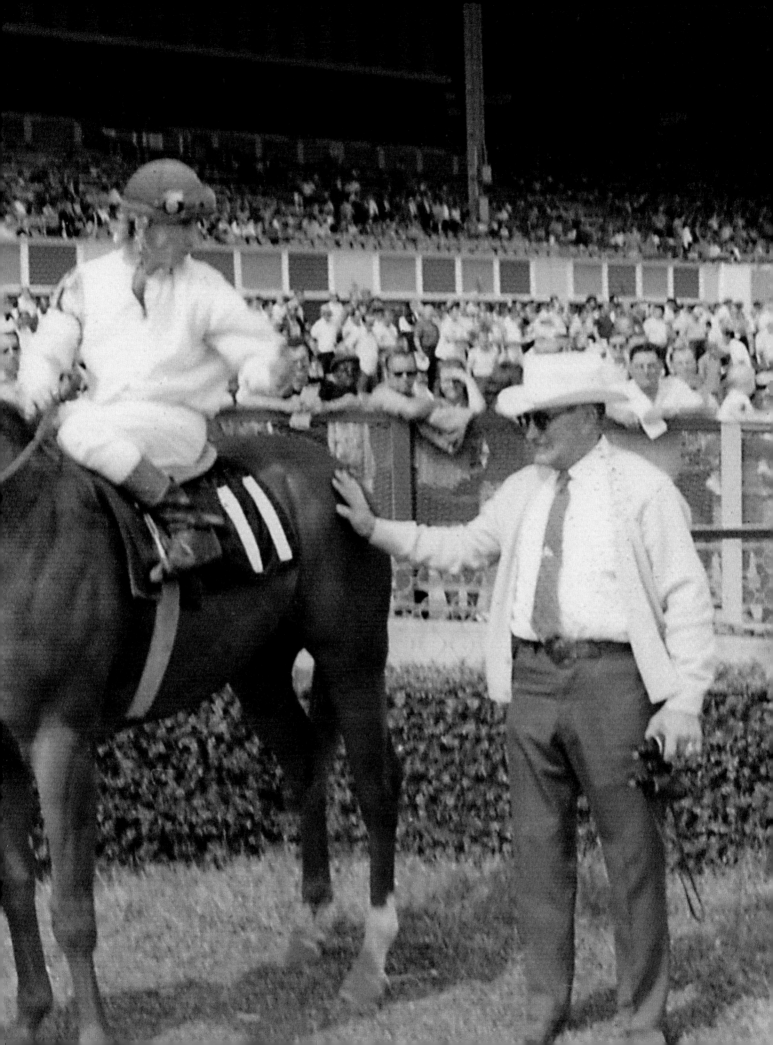

by Joe Buck

"I hope that this time I've spent in the hospital, going through all this, has taught you something. You have to live your life and let it go. Don't worry about things so much, and do what you want to do. Build your house, take trips with Ann, enjoy being with your kids. You never know, Buck, what's around the corner, you have to make the most of the time you've got. By the time you are in here, it's too late."

Those were some of the last words my father ever said to me. It was the beginning of March 2002, and I was about to leave for spring training. As you can imagine, I didn't want to go. My father had been in the hospital for over two months, and every day brought new complications that made his release seem less and less likely. Now he was facing major brain surgery, a radical measure to try to start the healing process that had been slowed by Parkinson's disease.

The Cardinals season was just about to officially start, and the goal we had all set for my dad now seemed unrealistic. From the time he entered the hospital in December for lung cancer surgery, we had all looked to the start of the baseball season as the time when everything would be all right. Things were not all right. My hesitation emotionally, and even physically, regarding my duties as the St. Louis Cardinals announcer, annoyed him. I felt like I was 12 years old again, about to leave for summer camp, knowing I would soon be miserable and homesick. Back then I feared that once I left, I might never see my mom and dad again. I imagined all sorts of terrible things happening as I was away swimming in

"I learned to love golf and got to be a pretty good player because of my dad. He loved golfing in his free time and always said he thought his job was perfect because he could go to the golf course in the morning, the race track in the afternoon and the ballpark in the evening."

—Joe

a lake in Missouri, unaware of some tragic event happening at home. The world seemed so scary outside of my little cocoon in Ladue, Missouri, and I didn't want to face it without holding my mom or dad's hand.

Those same feelings washed over me as I talked to my father in the intensive care unit at Barnes Hospital. I was about to leave for Florida, the same trip I had made and loved every year since 1969.

"I don't want to go, Dad. I want to stay with you and make sure everything's okay here," I said.

All he had to do was give me that look. He had a look that said it all. "C'mon, give me a break, you have to go, it's your job. Haven't I taught you anything? Be a man and get down there!"

All that from just a stare. What a face. It was the same stare that warned me to stop arguing with my mother about something insignificant, or to stop criticizing an umpire while we broadcast a game together, or to let me know that I had pulled off another "caper," staying out too late with my best friend in Florida. I knew what he was saying with that look, because you could tell what he was thinking at every turn. He freely shared his feelings with those around him. My dad was truly an open book, and he never hid how he felt about anything.

If you had any sense, all it took was a look from him to know if you had passed or failed. I think that was true of family, friends, and even fans to a certain extent. If you flipped on a Cardinals game at any point in the action, you could tell if the Cardinals were winning or losing just by the tone of his voice. He never had to say it; you just knew.

"While Jack was doing the morning show at KMOX, I would walk with Joe around downtown St. Louis. Around noon when Jack finished, he would join us and push the stroller for a while. On this trip, Joe and I encountered some children campaigning for an upcoming city election."

—Carole

As my dad reached his seventies, he allowed those feelings to flow out in the form of poetry. He used to joke that I would roll my eyes as he unveiled his latest work with unabashed enthusiasm. I think I initially reacted that way to his poetry because I felt that he kept nothing inside, nothing to himself, and I didn't understand why he needed to do that. I realize now that it was necessary for him to keep giving anything he could to make people think, to re-evaluate, and to learn through his experiences.

As his health began to fail, even before he entered the hospital for the final time, this outlet was vital to his existence. He needed to touch and to feel and to share with the people who filled his audience night after night, game after game. In the last ten or so years of his life, no matter where we were, my dad went out of his way to approach strangers, introduce himself and ask about their history. I believe he knew it all could end at any moment, and he wanted to take a count before he left. I think he really gained

strength from hearing stories recalled to him of things that had happened earlier in his life, when he was young and vibrant. He wanted to know that he had made a difference. It wasn't an ego thing; it was essential to keep him going. He kept very few things to himself, and it needed to be that way.

Do not misunderstand; my dad was a tough guy, who, if crossed, was not a "sit back and take it" kind of guy. I remember one night when I was little when my mom, my dad and I went to a Dairy Queen. Two teenagers were hanging out on the curb, smoking and making comments to passersby. As my mom and I walked in to get our dipped cones, the little critics directed a snide comment at my pretty mom. Unfortunately for them, they said it a little too loudly. When my dad heard them, he threw the car into drive, whipped around the corner and pulled up in front of the young citizens. He hopped out and gave them a piece of his mind just as my mom and I came toward the car. He smiled, got back in the car, and said to us, "I scared the hell out of them, didn't I?"

As I walked out of my dad's hospital room the night before leaving for spring training, the very last thing he said to me was, "Take care of your mother, okay?"

"I will, Dad, don't worry about that, I gotcha covered," I said.

I will, Dad.

— Joe ■

"Dad put all of the grandchildren through his 'bravery test.' It entailed perching them on top of the refrigerator and stepping away. If the child did not cry, he or she passed the test. Here, Joe's oldest daughter Natalie passes with flying colors despite the screams of her mother and grandmother to 'take that child down!'"

—Julie

"Five of my adorable grandchildren sit still long enough for a picture. Joe's two daughters Natalie [oldest] and Trudy pose with their cousins [from left] Jack, Ben and Matt, Julie's children."

—Carole

"Jack loved having his family at the ballpark. Here they are—the three Jacks."

—Carole

"I often spent time at the stadium with my father. Because of him, I got to meet a lot of interesting people, such as actor Gordon McRae [center] and Cardinals general manager Bing Devine."

—Joe

"In this photo, one of my favorites, I am learning to walk and a whole lot of other things with Dad in 1950. I knew and loved Dad for over half a century. I am blessed by the many riches he left me: a sense of humor, a strong work ethic and a true love of people. When our father called me 'Number One,' I knew it meant firstborn, and not number two, three, four, five, six, seven or eight, but it was fun to pretend it meant number one favorite. Our dad was a great parent and role model as he unconditionally loved all of his three sons and five daughters. He also loved his 16 grandchildren and the thousands of other children who needed him."

—Beverly

"Here are Danny, Joe, Jack and Jack Jr. having a good time and supporting a worthy cause at the annual Budweiser Guns 'n' Hoses event in St. Louis. Local police and firefighters square off in the ring for friendly boxing matches, and the proceeds support Backstoppers, an organization that assists the families of police officers and firefighters who lose their lives in the line of duty."

—Carole

Joe and Julie cuddle up for a photo opportunity.

"I married the love of my life."

by **Carole Buck**

"I gotcha covered like the morning dew."

Jack was almost bigger than life. If I was worried or fearful he could make the world go away. He was fun, unpredictable, sensitive, funny, busy, smart and handsome. How could one man possess all of these qualities? Well, he did.

If the world says you should give your wife a card or a present on Valentine's Day, he would get it done *his* way on *his* time. There would be pearls in a paper bag or a Christmas package sticking out of his pocket at the end of Christmas day.

Many times on winter evenings we would turn out the lights in the den and turn music on and not speak, letting the music evoke memories or dreams or peace—and he would sing along.

We had so many laughs at night. When the humidifier hummed a certain pitch, the fan was on and the windows were open (he always had the window open because of staying in so many hotel rooms), I would ask him to tell me a story. Sometimes in the later years he would make up a baseball team, using his medicines: "Sinemet is up to bat and Mirapex is on first," etc. Sometimes he would recite a new poem and I'd flip the light on, get a pencil and paper to listen and write, or we'd both sing the lyrics to a new country song. "She's

Happy Birthday, Carole

You are as much a part of me
as my dyskinesia

It's great to be married to you
I couldn't forget you if I had amnesia

But I'm puzzled by
one thing you do

I really don't know why you do it
most would call it perverse

But every year on the 18th of August
you celebrate your birthday in reverse

At one time I was 18 years older
people are easy to fool

But if the gap becomes any wider
you'll soon be going back to school

Happy Birthday to you, darling
it's tough to grow old I think

And, sadly, when I celebrate 80
you'll be too young to share a drink!

five-foot-five of trouble, trouble with a wandering eye, keeps me on the bubble, keeps me wondering why. I've seen her wink at strangers, flirt with another guy. She's five-foot-five of trouble, trouble with a wandering eye."

On Christmas Eve he sang a song for the Christmas program on KMOX. It went like this:

"Welcome to our house whoever you are.
Please come and join us, our loved ones are with us
as we retell the story of the Bethlehem star.
If you need a friend you have found one,
a shoulder to lighten your load.
Celebrate this Christmas
the greatest story ever told."

St. Louis football Cardinals Hall of Fame lineman Dan Dierdorf made a joke about Jack Buck's color-blindness. Buck was known to wear some loud outfits, even with wife Carole helping him to get the proper look.

"It was always a thrill to see him for the first time in a day," Dierdorf said.

Dierdorf recalled the time Buck showed up for work wearing a red jacket and orange pants. "He took one more step, stopped dead in his tracks, and said, 'Carole wasn't home,'" Dierdorf said.

The only time he didn't want to talk to people was in the morning when he ate his sweet roll and drank his coffee. It was almost as if the phone was not supposed to ring at that hour, and if it did that look would come across his face, a look that meant, "Run to your battle stations, the enemy is approaching!" That look could mean a lot of things. To the children it meant, "I don't like your grades," "Don't argue," or "What do you mean, you got a ticket?" To me it meant, "I just looked at the bills or the cancelled checks and you've gone too far." He used to say, "Blondie, I hope you don't ask for the moon, because I'd have to try to get it for you." Later he rethought that!

We had the same sense of humor. He could make me laugh! Many times when he read books at night he would read me different paragraphs that he particularly loved and sometimes I would say, "Turn the light off." He'd say, "Nobody is going to tell me when to turn the light off in my house." PAUSE. (Book thrown on the chair and the light turns off.)

SILENCE. "I'm sorry." "Me too. You know I wasn't afraid in the Second World War, but I'm afraid of you."

I was never a good cook, but he wasn't a good eater. He had a pacemaker and he used to tell people, "I know when she's mad at me because she turns on the microwave and calls me to the phone to answer a call. With a pacemaker you should never be within ten feet of the microwave. Well, the phone was next to the microwave!"

Once my mother Lillie, who was 80 years old at the time, was driving along a winding road in St. Louis County and careened around a curve and decapitated a fire hydrant, creating another wonder of the world—a geyser in St. Louis County. The water was shooting up a hundred feet. When the police arrived and the firemen jumped off the trucks, my mother looked at them and said, "I'm Jack Buck's mother-in-law; just send the bill to him." And they did. He said mothers-in-law are like seeds, they come with the tomato.

I married the love of my life, and he made me feel like I was the most beautiful woman he ever met. And it doesn't get any better than that.

— *Carole* ■

"Carole once asked me what I would say if I met the Lord, and my answer then is the same as it is now; I want to ask Him why He was so good to me."

— Jack Buck

*All-
American*

chapter
FIVE

The beginning of talk
radio and talk television
in this country started at
KMOX with a program
by the name of "At Your
Service" hosted by Jack.
During one of the pro-
grams for the show, Jack
interviewed Eleanor
Roosevelt, whom he said
was "a lovely lady."

"It meant a great deal to us when Commissioner Selig said that Dad's reading of his patriotic poem after the September 11 attacks restarted the game of baseball for America. Dad was proud to be an American and we were proud of him."

—Julie

Since this nation was founded, under God
More than 200 years ago
We have the bastion of freedom
The light that keeps the free world aglow
We do not covet the possessions of others
We are blessed with the bounty we share

We have rushed to help other nations, anything, anytime, anywhere.

War is just not our nature
We won't start, but we will end the fight
If we are involved we shall be resolved
To protect what we know is right.

We have been challenged by a cowardly foe
Who strikes and then hides from our view
With one voice we say, "There is no choice today,
There is only one thing to do."

Everyone is saying the same thing and praying
That we end these senseless moments we are living
As our fathers did before, we shall win this unwanted war
And our children will enjoy the future we'll be giving.

Jack delivered this poem
after the tragic events of
September 11, 2001

THE WHITE HOUSE

WASHINGTON

December 22, 1989

Dear Jack:

It was great to welcome you and all the sports
announcers and writers who came for the recent briefing
at the White House. I relished the informal discussion
on America's favorite pastime -- and particularly about
this past season.

I prize the personalized "St. Louis Cardinals" jacket
and those baseballs autographed by Whitey Herzog and
Ozzie Smith; and that handsome Cardinal ornament is
on our personal Christmas tree. Many thanks, Jack,
for these special mementos.

Barbara joins me in sending you our best wishes,

Sincerely,

Gy Bush

Mr. Jack Buck
14 Overbrook Drive
St. Louis, Missouri 63124

The President
requests the pleasure of your company
at a reception to be held at
The White House
Tuesday afternoon, July 22, 1969
at 4:00 o'clock

To Jack Buck
With best wishes,

Ronald Reagan

GEORGE BUSH

WASHINGTON
November 1, 1992
(aboard Air Force One)

Dear Jack,

I just want to thank you for being at our rally in Saint
Louis. It meant a great deal to everyone there and it
certainly meant much to me.

I am most grateful for your support and appreciate your
willingness to stand up there at a critical time. Many,
many thanks.

Warm best wishes,

One of Jack's favorite charitable organizations was the Cystic Fibrosis Foundation. He served as chief fundraising chairman of the local chapter since the mid-1960s, raising millions of dollars. He was very generous with his time and rarely turned down a speaking engagement. Carole remembers that Jack would often prepare his speech during the dinner portion of the evening, as seen in this photo, and deliver it perfectly.

A Civic

Mind

Mike Roarty

An Anheuser-Busch executive for nearly four decades, Mike Roarty developed the aggressive sports marketing strategy that established Anheuser-Busch as the No. 1 beer producer in the world. Buck and Roarty met in the early 1970s, when Roarty was in charge of Cardinals broadcasts for the brewery, beginning a close friendship that lasted more than 30 years.

"Jack lived here in St. Louis and he was a well-known figure in many circles. When it came to charities, Jack couldn't say no, so he presided at something like 200 dinners or lunches a year for charitable causes.

He was very much a man of community, doing everything he could to help. This was especially true for children's causes.

He knew hard times, as he used to say. It wasn't easy. He was raised in a large family, a very close family. His mother was the principle figure in that family.

He had great respect and affection for his father. He could relate to people who were down on their luck. That had a lot to do with his very generous tipping habits. I knew him for many years, and everywhere he went he was a generous tipper. He made everyone's day; you could measure that by the bright smiles and the attention that our party would get because of his tipping.

It made it a little difficult for people like me who insist on paying our share and picking up the tab every other time. Because of Jack, people would expect beyond a twenty percent tip. Jack was far more generous than that. He'd go around and see that people were properly rewarded. He was an incredible, generous, good guy.

Office of the Mayor

City of Saint Louis

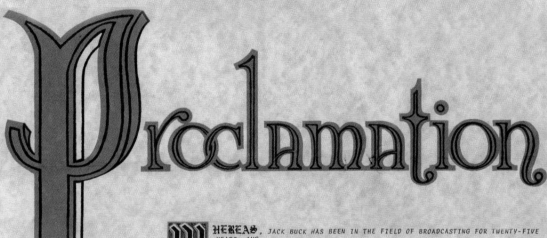

Proclamation

WHEREAS, JACK BUCK HAS BEEN IN THE FIELD OF BROADCASTING FOR TWENTY-FIVE YEARS; AND

WHEREAS, IN THAT TIME HE HAS ACTED AS AN AMBASSADOR FOR THE GREAT CITY OF SAINT LOUIS SPREADING THE CIVIC MESSAGE AS HE TRAVELS THROUGHOUT THE COUNTRY; AND

WHEREAS, HE HAS CONTRIBUTED HIS TIME, EFFORT AND TALENTS TO A NUMBER OF CHARITIES, ORGANIZATIONS AND BUSINESSES IN THE CITY OF SAINT LOUIS:

NOW, THEREFORE, I, JAMES F. CONWAY, MAYOR OF THE CITY OF SAINT LOUIS, DO HEREBY PROCLAIM JUNE 15-21, 1980, AS

JACK BUCK WEEK

IN THE CITY OF SAINT LOUIS AS A TRIBUTE TO HIS DEDICATION, CONTRIBUTIONS AND TALENTS.

IN WITNESS WHEREOF, I HAVE HEREUNTO SET MY HAND AND CAUSED TO BE AFFIXED THE SEAL OF THE CITY OF SAINT LOUIS, THIS 17th DAY OF June , A.D., 1980.

Attest

James F. Conway
Mayor of the City of Saint Louis

Dorothy Whalen
Register

Mayor Conway honored Jack in 1980 for his diverse and abundant contributions to the city of St. Louis.

We went to Ireland several times for the Budweiser Irish Derby in June every year. Jack would look forward to that trip; it was a time to get a little rest in leading up to the All-Star Game. It was a few days where he could relax comfortably and enjoy Ireland, which he did thoroughly.

He just loved going over there. The Irish have a unique sense of humor, and Jack enjoyed that very much. His mother's people came from Ireland, up around the Dingle Peninsula. He had a great time visiting that region.

We went to Normandy and he walked among all of those white crosses. Jack was an emotional guy who would cry easily at things that touched his heart. At that cemetery that day, he wandered into a corner to have a good private cry by himself. As we went back to Paris in the car, he wrote a poem about that experience.

Jack was such a public figure that I think most people are very much aware of his "tell it like it is" sports reporting. Jack didn't believe in castigating the fellow who made a mistake or who didn't perform up to his usual level.

He felt that like any other human being, they deserved a little more compassion, a little understanding. You'd never hear him rip a player or his performance on a given day.

One way for Jack to give to the community was to play in celebrity softball games. Here, Jack (top row, second from the right) is shown with one of those teams, along with Minnesota Fats and his world-famous pool cue (top row, far left).

Conversely, Harry Caray would. Harry was famous for what people called his bombastic description of the game and who was playing. They were a good contrast working together.

Jack factually reported the incident or the play but did not criticize the performer in harsh terms. If a player made a mistake, he reported that accurately, but he didn't go into anything beyond that.

I think most people would understand after knowing Jack and listening to him all these years, when he described a play or gave an opinion on something, it was always objective and fair.

Jack stopped doing Cardinals broadcasts at one point in the 1970s to host a show called *Grandstand* on NBC. The nature of St. Louis fans is to support the people they really like. They liked Jack immensely.

He was an incredibly popular figure, so if he went on to become a national figure with the network, I think they still would be claiming him as a hometown boy, even though he wasn't born here. He was so much a part of the community up until that time. I think he will stand as probably the most cherished broadcaster and

Jack was passionate about the St. Louis community. In fact, Jack once spoke at 385 engagements in one year. "Every time more than 10 people sat down to eat, I was there talking to them," he joked.

In 1969, Jack organized a charity golf tournament to benefit the Cystic Fibrosis Foundation and the tradition has endured. 2003 marks the 34th Annual Jack Buck Golf Classic. His tournament attracts more than 300 golfers every year and has raised over $7 million for Cystic Fibrosis research.

communicator of sports in this community. That'll last at least a generation. He won't be easily forgotten.

Jack had just been named Citizen of the Year by the city fathers. That was a great tribute to Jack. He stepped away from the microphone at the Missouri Athletic Club the evening of the banquet and went directly to the hospital. You know the rest.

Jack's calls kind of became hallmarks for him. We were out at a restaurant after a Rams game downtown and you could hear people every once in a while say, "That's a winner," or "Go crazy, folks!" It's very much a prominent part of his legacy.

He was a unique individual whose heart was as big as Busch Stadium and everybody loved him for it. ■

Jack and Bill Cosby shared a great deal in common— their unique senses of humor, their involvement with charitable organizations and their commitment to children.

Just One Moment

I saw a kid in a wheelchair today,
and he deeply affected me.
He was on the field at a baseball game,
and was a gut-wrenching sight to see.

I would guess his age at 11 or so,
his body was twisted and bent,
palsy has clutched him since the day he was born
and dictated the life he has spent.

His mother and father were there with him;
this was not the picture she dreamed.
They watched the players hit, run and throw,
and weren't jealous, or so it seemed.

I looked at the grass, the sun and the sky,
and pondered the beauties of earth.
And wondered how often he asks why
and what he thinks life is worth?

This little guy couldn't walk or talk,
when he shook his head "no" it meant "yes."
How much he knows of what others go through,
is anybody's guess.

His dad held him up so he could see,
a slugger hit it a mile.
Then a hero gave him an autographed ball,
and all he could do was smile.

In 1988, Jack was named the St. Louis Variety Club Champion for Kids. Here he is with a young friend and fellow KMOX announcer Jay Randolph at the annual Variety Club Telethon.

CBS Radio Sports

From the

chapter
SEVEN

Hank Stram and Jack were football broadcast partners for CBS Radio from 1978 to 1996. They broadcast numerous Super Bowls together and were great friends outside the booth. Hank remembered, "[Jack] never met a stranger. He liked people very much. He was always kind and generous."

Gridiron

The Pro Football Hall of Fame honored Jack in 1996 with the Pete Rozelle Award (left) for "exceptional longtime contributions to radio and TV in pro football." In 1976, Jack did the play-by-play for the first professional football game played outside the United States when the Cardinals played the San Diego Chargers in Japan.

Hank Stram

The winningest head coach in the 10-year history of the American Football League, Hank Stram joined Jack Buck in the CBS radio booth in 1978. Together, they called Monday Night games and Super Bowls from 1978 through 1996.

"We first got acquainted when Jack was doing games for ABC with Paul Christman. I was working for the Dallas Texans in the old American Football League. I worked for television and radio and I got a call from Jim Finks in Chicago one day.

"CBS called," he said. "They're going to have a Monday night radio show and they asked me to recommend somebody, so I recommended you. Would you be interested in it?"

"Yeah," I said. "Sure I'd be interested in it."

"Oh, great," he said, "here's the number; call them and tell them you're interested."

So I called them back, told them that I'd be interested in it.

"Well, how would you like to work with Jack Buck?" they said.

"Well, gee, that'd be fine," I said. "I know Jack from the days he was with ABC and that'd be wonderful."

The basic thing about Jack was that I always considered him to be a baseball announcer. That's how I remembered him when I grew up and in the early stages of my life. When we got together on CBS radio and television, it was amazing to me how alert he was and how much he knew about football.

I found out while I was doing broadcasting with him that he always wanted to go down and see the officials before the game. So I'd go down there with him and visit with the officials.

I found out at that time that he was once a football official for high schools, colleges, the whole thing. I was amazed that he had that kind of background.

So we're doing games together, and it was amazing to me how many times officials would get confused as to what really happened on a certain play when they called timeout.

Before they could say it, Jack would say on the air that this is what happened, this is what the problem was, blah blah blah.

I was always amazed in his ability and I finally realized that it was because of his training. He did basketball. He did football. He did baseball. But I always looked upon him as a baseball guy.

We did the championship game between Dallas and the 49ers in San Francisco the year that the 49ers beat Dallas with the big catch at the end of the game with Montana throwing to Dwight Clark.

Clark caught the ball in the end zone and they won the game. That was a very exciting game and Jack and I did it together. It will always linger in my book of great memories with regard to a football game.

One of Jack's "duties" when he was broadcasting football for CBS was to go to Hawaii for the Pro Bowl. Here, he is clowning around poolside at the Royal Hawaiian Hotel with fellow broadcasters Hank Stram (bottom) and Brent Musburger (right) and producer Bill Ceverha (left).

Every time we went up into the booth, he'd come in with a bag of Snickers candy bars and throw it onto the counter by the telephone. If he made a move of some kind, I'd hurry and get over to the bag and grab a Snickers or two and put them in my pocket, because I like Snickers too.

This one day, he goes up to the top of the press box with some friends. I'm there with the telephone and the TV set and everything. I saw the candy bars and I grabbed one of them. I took the package off and grabbed it and took a bite. It was part of the instrument for our TV set!

He saw me do it. I thought I was going to break all the teeth in my mouth and he was up there laughing. He got the biggest kick out of that. All those people up there were laughing at it.

I was looking around, and there he was up there laughing his head off because he pulled a fast one on me regarding Snickers. Man, I thought I broke all my teeth.

I used to kid him a little bit. I called him Skippy because he liked peanut butter.

He didn't like to be called Skippy. So we're doing a TV game in Cleveland and one of the engineers for the TV station there came over.

Pat Summerall presents Jack with one of his many distinguished service awards. Pat and Jack teamed up for several football broadcasts in the 1960s. Summerall later remembered, "I learned from Jack that there's a place in the game for humor, that we were not broadcasting from Westminster Abbey. Jack was always loose about things. Before a game would start, he'd look over at me and say, 'You don't think I'm ready, do you?' But he always was. He just liked to have fun."

"Hey, Coach, you know what?" he said. "I get the feeling that Jack Buck doesn't like to be called Skippy."

"No, no," I said. "It's a term of endearment. He loves it, he just loves it."

"Well, I want to make sure," he said, "because when I go down and talk to him I have to interview him like I have to interview you before the game, and I just want to make sure I don't make any mistakes."

"No, no," I told him. "Just call him Skippy and he knows it's just a term of endearment and he knows you like him. Don't worry about it."

Afterwards, the kid comes running back up.

"Hey, Coach," he says, "you know, Skippy was really mad at me for calling him Skippy. He called me some of the worst names I've ever heard in my life. He didn't like to be called Skippy."

"Well, you must have mispronounced what you were saying," I said. "Normally, that wouldn't be a problem."

"Oh, he was very, very upset," he told me.

We had a lot of fun. We enjoyed each other very, very much. We worked together very smoothly. There were never any problems. That's the way it was.

There isn't a day that he doesn't pop into my mind and I remember some of the things that we did together. He was an artist and took great pride in what he did and how he did it.

It was never a haphazard thing. It was always preparation. He was well prepared; he knew what he was going to say and how he was going to say it and all that kind of stuff. But he was so spontaneous that you never knew what to expect because he came out with great one-liners and all that kind of stuff.

"There's the snap; there's the kick. It is up; it is...no good! Norwood missed! Four seconds left. The Giants have won Super Bowl XXV by the score of 20-19."

— Jack's famous call from the final seconds of the Super Bowl on January 27, 1991.

He could be in the midst of a group talking about a variety of different things, and somebody would ask him to give a speech at the podium and he'd leave and do the greatest job you've ever heard in your life.

He was always very kind and generous to people. We'd go out to dinner and people would come over to us and talk about one thing or the other. We'd send them over part of the meal or a steak or a beer or whatever it might be.

We had so many things in common. We played golf together. We were always together and had a lot of fun in conjunction with that. Our wives got along, my Phyllis and his Carole.

We did the Pro Bowl; we did Super Bowls together. It was a very, very close relationship, and I considered myself very, very lucky to be able to be associated with Jack for those years.

I was very lucky that I was able to spend that much time with Jack Buck, and it just broke my heart when I found out about his illness. I called Stan Musial all the time while he was in the hospital.

I couldn't get his wife Carole because she was busy at the hospital too, so I called Stan Musial to find out about Jack. And he would tell me what his condition was, and it was always a big concern because every indication pointed to the fact that he wasn't going to live much longer.

All of the sudden I got a call that he had passed away. But now young Joe is following in his footsteps. He's going to be a superstar, I guarantee it. He's terrific. ▪

Jack talks baseball with the legendary
Jackie Robinson on "At Your Service."

Talkin'

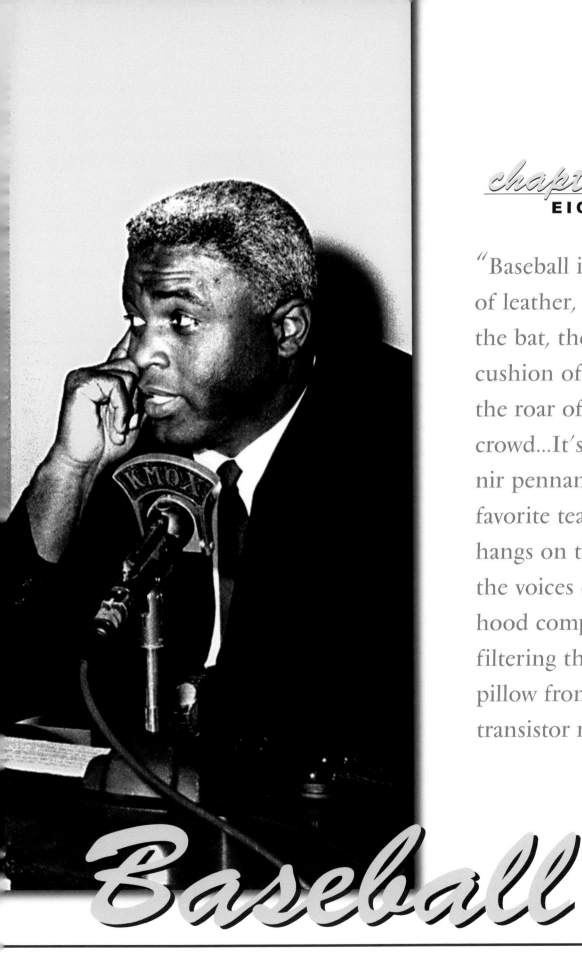

chapter
EIGHT

"Baseball is the smell of leather, the crack of the bat, the bumpy cushion of grass and the roar of the crowd...It's the souvenir pennant of your favorite team that still hangs on the wall. It's the voices of our childhood companions filtering through our pillow from that transistor radio."

Baseball

Bill Gainey

The following essay was penned by one of Jack's colleagues at KMOX, Bill Gainey, a former account executive. Bill's words so captured the spirit of our national pastime that Jack recorded the piece for one of his broadcasts. We are proud to reprint those words here.

" It's the great American pastime—baseball. It's not just a game invented for athletes who can run from home to first in four seconds, or throw a ball 90 miles an hour, or hit a ball over the fence. It's a game made for kids and played by kids and those who still have a lot of "little kid" inside them. And it's more than just a game.

More than anything else, baseball is memories—memories pressed between the pages of my mind. It's Lou Gehrig's farewell speech at Yankee Stadium, echoing in the minds of everyone who was there—or wishes they had been there. It's Bobby Thompson's dramatic ninth-inning home run against Brooklyn and the memory of Russ Hodges's play-by-play. It's

Being in the Cardinals' broadcast booth for nearly half a century gave Jack the opportunity to interview many of the all-time great players, such as Mickey Mantle (above) and Hank Aaron (right).

every kid who ever went to bed with a transistor radio tucked beneath their pillow listening to the game and pretending to be asleep when their parents came in to check on them before the parents went to their own bedroom to finish listening to the game.

Even more than all that, it's our own memories of our own "field of dreams." We are all Kevin Costner playing catch again with his departed father. That's why, to me or any other baseball fan, the story isn't about baseball or cornfields or a wish come true; it's about family. The real pull is father-child.

Throughout this century, baseball has grown into a painless means of bringing abrasive generations together smoothly. Remember how much fun it was to hit your dad's pitching and watch while he chased the ball? It's not often the parent does the chore for the child any more. As a teenager, it was a relief to use the ballpark as a demilitarized zone during generation gap hostilities over politics, grades, clothes, cars, haircuts, music. As a young adult, talking baseball was a reliable way to cut through long absences and put a homecoming on solid, diamond-hard ground. Now as we become parents ourselves, the force of these signposts can be doubled as we go through the same drills with our children.

There is certainly something unique about baseball that produces these "happenings." The father-child bond could be welded over cards or car mechanics. What *is* special about an activity like baseball is that so many families have been tied to it for so many decades. It has been and still remains the most common denominator for most of us.

Remember the kid who was so thrilled to get his first baseball bat at Christmas? He couldn't wait to take it outside and play pepper. He held it as

Pirates Hall of Famer Willie Stargell was one of Jack's favorite ballplayers. Stargell's swing-and-a-miss sealed Bob Gibson's no-hitter on August 14, 1971 and Jack was on his feet, screaming into the microphone and crying tears of joy while he called the final pitch.

carefully as a Nintendo joystick, took a couple of practice swings and clicked on a smile that would light up an Iowa cornfield at midnight. Then he fungoed an easy grounder to his old man, who was wearing a battered catcher's mitt given to him so many years ago by *his* father.

Baseball is the smell of leather, the crack of the bat, the bumpy cushion of grass and the roar of the crowd—hot dogs, beer, soda, popcorn, peanuts, crackerjacks. It's the souvenir pennant of your favorite team that still hangs on the wall. It's the voices of our childhood companions filtering through our pillow from that transistor radio. What made all these memories was the sum of all those baseball sensations, divided by two—a father and his child.

There is still nothing, anywhere, to beat it. I don't know about you, but I'd give anything to play catch just one more time with my dad.

Jack's busy schedule forced him to maximize his free time, like on long plane rides, to write speeches and prepare for broadcasts.

Jack talks baseball with Hall of Fame manager Sparky Anderson.

Jack pauses for a photo with some of his favorite Cardinals from the 1992 team: Andres Galarraga (left), Ozzie Smith (middle) and Pedro Guerrero (right).

AP/WWP

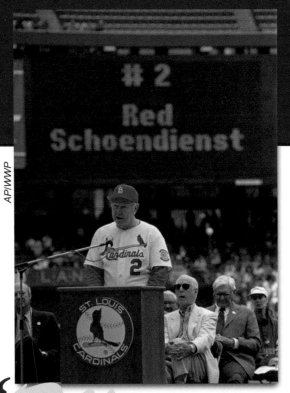

Jack was on hand to help honor his friend at Busch Stadium when the team retired Red Schoendienst's jersey.

Red Schoendienst

Red was one of Jack's best friends, both in and out of baseball. He managed the Cardinals for 12 years and currently serves as a coach. Schoendienst was the skipper for the world champion Redbirds in 1967.

"With Jack, there were so many memories. He was talented, not only broadcasting, but meeting people. He was never a stranger. Traveling with him in baseball, at restaurants and everywhere we went, well, he'd see people there and he'd just about know everyone. It was a pleasure to be around him.

Jack and I got to be great friends because of all the time we spent together on the road. When we went to New York, we would go to stage shows and plays. Any time we had a chance we would make sure to see the best shows. We usually knew someone who had some tickets. One night we took a cab to the theatre, and after it was over, we came out and would you believe the same guy that dropped us off picked us up. I said, "Now this is unusual, Jack." I thought that maybe he had it planned for the guy to pick us up at a certain time, because that was just like him, but he said, "No. It was just a strange coincidence."

Jack and Stan Musial and I went out one night to see *The Pajama Game* when it first was on Broadway. When we were with Jack, we always went backstage after the show and saw all the stars. And that was always a big, big thing for us. Jack was so well known, even in New York.

Jack was also well read. He was up on everything. When he was doing a banquet, he was the best emcee that I know of. When he would introduce somebody, maybe at a writers' dinner or something, he always had a story about them. Jack always had a story about everybody. Jack could make you laugh no matter what.

One thing about him, whether he was on the air or eating in a restaurant, he never used any coarse words that you shouldn't use. He was just that kind of guy—good manners were very important to him.

Even though he probably had some good insight about baseball, he never criticized my managing. I managed the Cardinals for 12 years and never heard a word of criticism about me or anyone else. He was very considerate.

I've also never heard a better guy in interviewing. I don't care who he was interviewing; he could always keep the interview going. Jack would never bug anybody to do an interview, either. He would go up to them, and I saw him do it a number of times, and he would ask, "Do you mind? Can I take some of your time and interview you at your convenience?" So when he interviewed a guy, it was always at the guy's own convenience.

Don't get me wrong, Jack could play a few tricks on you once in a while, but nothing that could harm

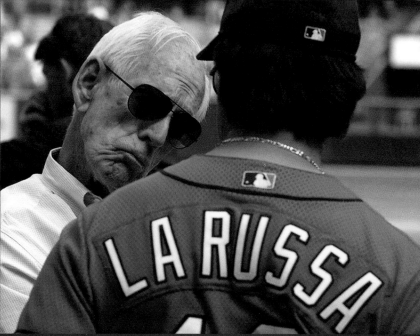

Jack often interviewed his good friend, Cardinals manager Tony La Russa, such as after this June 2001 game at Busch Stadium. Jack described La Russa as the General Patton of baseball, because of his intensity and his drive to win.

AP/WWP

Jack congratulates the team during the post-championship banquet in 1964. Jack partnered with Harry Caray to send the thrilling World Series action over the radio waves. The Cardinals faced Yankee sluggers Mickey Mantle and Roger Maris and were severely out-pitched, but won a well-deserved championship in seven games.

you—only things to make you laugh. He had a tremendous sense of humor.

He had a magnetic personality, too. People flocked to him and he always made them feel welcome. Once we saw Jonathan Winters in San Francisco at a restaurant. Winters was there with about a dozen of his people—doing an awards show or a benefit or something. When he saw his old schoolmate from Ohio State, he joined our group and sat with us the whole night.

Jack was a self-made man and he worked hard in his day. He was a legend in St. Louis and really drew a crowd. If you wonder why the St. Louis Cardinals have such a great following in baseball, well, it's partly because of the great announcers we have had all the way down the line—Harry Caray, Jack Buck, Mike Shannon. They bring you the game, and

Jack and Stan Musial were longtime friends. They golfed together in the summer and lived near each other in St. Louis. Jack said, "Musial is still the greatest player to ever wear a Cardinals uniform."

Jack knew how to bring it. Even when he was doing football, he and Hank Stram were the best I ever heard.

One of my lasting impressions of him is from when he first came to the Cardinals. He would be sitting on the team plane just across from or behind me, and he would be reading. Jack could read a book quicker than anybody I've ever seen.

We all really miss having Jack around. If he could come back for just a day, I would tell him, "Great to see you, so glad you're back." And I know that his response right then and there would be, "I'm the luckiest guy in the world."

Whatever Jack did was first class. ▄

Jack and Whitey Herzog were great friends and occasionally decent actors, such as when they made a Budweiser commercial spoofing the movie *Jaws*.

"Brock takes the lead, Ruthven checks him. He is going; the pitch is a strike; the throw is there! He did it! 105 for Lou Brock! About 50 ushers are on the field. The Cardinals pour out of the dugout to shake hands with their teammate—Reggie Smith, Ted Simmons, Bake McBride, Ken Reitz. All of the Cardinals—out of the dugout, out of the bullpen—mobbing Lou Brock, a fellow they dearly love on this Cardinal ballclub."

—Jack's call of Lou Brock's 105th stolen base in 1974.

Brock finished his 19-year career with 893 stolen bases, and Jack was on hand to congratulate him.

Lou Brock
#893

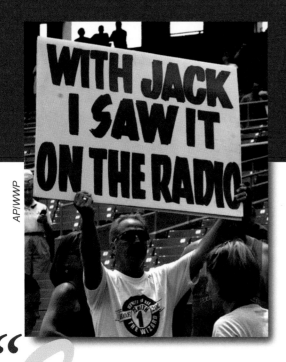

AP/WWP

"Working with Jack was the biggest thrill of my professional life."

Randy Karraker

Former KMOX sports anchor Randy Karraker worked with Jack Buck in a variety of capacities during their years together at the station (1983-2001). Karraker now hosts a sports talk show on KTRS in St. Louis.

"I started as an intern at KMOX in 1983 and actually had my first chance to work with Jack when I produced some Cardinals road games in 1984. I worked with him there and produced a lot of the shows that he did on KMOX in the 1980s. In the '90s, once I got on the air, I was able to co-host a lot of the open line shows with him until I left, which was April 2001.

The reason I got into the business was because I grew up listening to Jack. He influenced most of the people in broadcasting in St. Louis to get into the business. Working with him was the biggest thrill of my professional life. The greatest thing about it was that everything you imagine somebody being, he was all that and more.

He was the consummate professional. He was without question the best at what he did. He was the best baseball broadcaster. He was the best football broadcaster. He was the best at doing a talk show.

When Robert Hyland was alive, Jack was the final voice as the sports director. He was the one who made the decisions when somebody was hired. He was the one who put his

OPPOSITE PAGE: Jack hams it up with his bronze statue on the day of its unveiling at Busch Stadium on August 30, 1998. The statue honors Jack's longtime service as the Cardinals broadcaster. The plaque on the statue reads: "This statue features Jack in his favorite spot—behind the microphone. 'The Voice of the Cardinals' has broadcast more than 6,500 games. Member of 11 Halls of Fame, including shrines for baseball, football and radio. One of the all-time greats, he has broadcast all sports. St. Louis' top emcee is known for his great sense of humor and charitable work. 'The Voice of Summer,' he was the ticket to the game for those who could not be here."

final stamp of approval on it. Jack was not only the sports director in name, he was the sports director in action, too.

When you got in a room with him and found out what sort of a person he was, that's what really made it special. He was beyond reproach as a person. He was funny. He didn't have a mean bone in his body. He was nice to everybody. And that's what was really impressive about him.

For doing little things like running his board at a radio station, he'd pull a $50 bill out. Or if you engineered for him it was a $50 or a $100 bill almost all the time. He was extremely generous with everybody—with the cleaning people at the station, with production people who would help him cut a commercial. He would take money out of his pocket and be so generous to everybody.

Unlike a lot of broadcasters, as a veteran broadcaster, you could tell he really wanted young people to do well. He would do anything he could to help you out.

He played a big part in me getting on the air. He went to Mr. Hyland and said, "Hey, this guy knows what he's talking about. He's doing a great job for us; why don't you give him a chance on the air?"

In 1997 when I wound up doing those Cardinals games, he was the driving force behind that. He told some people that he thought I should do it and I got the chance. From an administrative standpoint, he had a great ear for talent and knew what talented people could do for the station.

From a professionalism standpoint, this town is different from many. In most cities, when you have sports talk radio, it's shock and jock talk and things like that. I think in St. Louis, because of Jack, we have a heightened sense of professionalism and gentleness. I don't think that

AP/WWP

being shocking or trying to talk down to listeners goes over as well in St. Louis as it does in some other markets, because of Jack.

The day after he died, the *Post-Dispatch* ran a great headline. It said he was the soul of the city. There's no question about that. We talk about him from a sports standpoint, but he was the true voice of St. Louis. KMOX bills itself as the voice of St. Louis, but Jack Buck was the voice of St. Louis.

When St. Louis was building that dome for the Rams, the people who were in charge of it hired Jack to do some commercials for them. What had been a rather unpopular idea suddenly became something that St. Louisans took to. They voted in the county for that dome, and he was a big part of why we got the Rams here.

From a national standpoint, when Jack read his poem after September 11, 2001, it was shown on all of the national TV networks and ESPN. That kind of brought St. Louis back and made us realize we should be here.

He was our spokesman. He was such a great gauge of how people in this community felt and he was able to reflect that.

He was beyond KMOX. For our entire community here in St. Louis, he was the guy who spoke for us. ■

During Jack's recovery from surgery, fans were invited to sign KMOX's giant get-well card at the Cardinals' home opener against the Colorado Rockies on April 1, 2002.

AP/WWP

BASEBALL

When someone asks you your favorite sport,
And you answer, "Baseball," in a blink,
There are certain qualities you must possess
And you're more taxed than you think.

In the frozen grip of winter,
I'm sure you'll agree with me,
Not a day goes by without someone
Talking baseball to some degree.

The calendar flips on New Year's Day.
The Super Bowl comes and it goes.
Get the other sports out of the way;
The green grass and the fever grows.

They start the campaign;
Pomp and pageantry reign.
You claim the pennant on Opening Day.

From April 'til Fall,
You'll follow the bouncing white ball.
Your team is set to go all the way.

It'll be hot dogs for dinner,
Six months of heaven, a winner.
Yes, baseball has always been it.

You would amaze all your friends
If they knew to what ends
You'd go for a little old hit.

The best times you've had
Have been with your mom and your dad
And a bat and a ball and a glove.

From the first time you played
To the last time you prayed,
It's been a simple matter of love.

Jack shares a laugh with St. Louis manager Ken Boyer and outfielder Lou Brock during a postgame interview.

Jack once said, "I enjoy being around people who are smarter than I am, and Whitey definitely falls into that group."

Whitey Herzog

Whitey Herzog and Jack Buck became close friends during Whitey's tenure as manager of the Cardinals (1980-90), and their friendship continued long after Herzog retired.

"I first met Jack when he came over to my hometown of New Athens, Illinois when they honored me and named the ball field there after me. He was there with Bing Devine, Jim Toomey and a lot of Cardinals people. It was during the late 1970s, when I was managing the Royals.

When I came to St. Louis, I think he was pretty disgruntled with the way things had gone the last 12 years or so. He told me one time that if we hadn't come back and played like we did in 1981 he was going to retire as a broadcaster. We did a radio show together five days a week for 10 years, and that's hard to do. He always had something good to ask me, and he just made it easy for me to do the show because of his professionalism.

When you talk about Cardinal tradition, you think about the great personalities. When I came here and got to know the Musials, the Schoendiensts, the Bucks and the Broegs on a more personal basis I just couldn't believe what good people they were.

We had some great times doing commercials together, and the one with us on the boat for Busch beer turned out to be a real hit. We filmed it down in Orlando, and even though we did it a long time ago, I still see pictures of us on the boat whenever I go to charity auctions and dinners.

In the commercial I threw a can of beer into the water and then a shark came and got it. Jack started up the motor. He didn't look very at ease in that boat—I don't know if he had ever fished before. Then they had a shark coming after it. It was something.

Jack and Harry Caray call a Cardinals game sans shirts in the hot sun at old Sportsman's Park.

He came to my 70th birthday party when he was really sick, and then he had to go to a parade after that. He said an awful lot of nice things. He was just a prince of a guy.

Even when he was suffering from Parkinson's, he was able to make a joke of it. He always had his wit and his senses. He never really let the Parkinson's bother him publicly. The night they had the celebration at the Fox Theater for the St. Louis sports century he was walking around backstage and had his hands in his pockets. He was kind of shaking, and I asked him what he was doing. He said, "I'm exercising my Parkinson's." He was always saying something like that. That was Jack for you.

I went to the Ambassador's Club luncheon when he was honored as the Man of the Year several years ago, and I couldn't believe all of the things Jack had done. He emceed every banquet, every program, and never charged anybody a nickel. I couldn't believe he had not been the Man of the Year before that. It was almost amazing to me.

OPPOSITE PAGE: Jack talks baseball with former spitball pitcher Heinie Meine and former Cardinals and Browns broadcaster France Laux in the studio at KMOX. *Photo provided by Ted Patterson.*

I don't think there was a luncheon or some other type of function that went on in St. Louis where Jack Buck wasn't the emcee. He never had an off day; he was busy every day. He was busier than I was, or any of the players.

I didn't see him after he went in the hospital, but Stan Musial would keep me posted because he could get into the hospital. When Jack died, people said it was a big loss, but I think that after what he went through the last five months or so it was kind of a blessing.

He was really a Cardinal fan. A lot of times I thought he took losses worse than I did. His face would be drawn, he would be down, and I'd ask, "What's the matter?" knowing that he was upset because we had lost. That was especially true in his later years. I'd say, "We'll get them tomorrow," or "We've just got to play better tomorrow," or something like that and he would perk up a little bit. But he would really take a loss really hard. He was such a great fan and loved the Cardinals so much. ■

Cardinals mascot Fredbird leads a group of Little Leaguers past the center field wall where groundskeepers cut the initials JFB to honor Jack during the June 19th game against the Angels. *AP/WWP*

JFB

chapter NINE

"He was so distinctive. And his calls were so simple sometimes. Just that one call: 'I don't believe what I just saw,' when [Kirk] Gibson hit that home run. What a great way to describe it. That's Jack's style. And it's that kind of thing, I think, that endeared Jack, not only to base-ball fans, just to people."

— Bob Ueker

"*That's a*

Winner!"

"When McGwire hit the 62nd home run in '98, we were all there watching Jack stand and applaud, a man who had seen everything, and there were tears coming down from his eyes."
— Broadcaster Chip Caray

Bob Broeg

Bob Broeg is the former sports editor of the St. Louis Post-Dispatch *and a member of the writer's wing of the Baseball Hall of Fame. Along with Rob Rains, Broeg co-authored Jack Buck's autobiography,* Jack Buck: "That's a Winner!"

"

Take my word that this Hall of Famer of baseball, football, and microphone could have been many things. Listening to the words flow, flavored with wit, warmth and wisdom, I can see him performing Clarence Darrow as a lawyer, basically defending and not prosecuting, because he was for the underdog in fact and finances.

He would have been a great lawyer. He would have been a great speaker, because when he accepted the Citizen of the Year award about two years ago, his acceptance was a masterpiece. It was the best I've ever heard, and he could have been an orator because he had that light touch. If he had decided to use a scalpel, he would have been a hell of a doctor, too. He was a talent and a much-loved man.

Buck had to be persuaded to write an autobiography. It is really the third-person recollections of a third-person guy. If it is an oxymoron, the man is a liberal conservative, meaning one who is proud to have lifted himself and encourages others, yet remains soft and sentimental.

He would probably cry at the National Anthem or, as he sometimes cracked, when cutting the ribbon at a supermarket opening. I do know that when he softly sang "Danny Boy," everyone else was crying as well.

I think Jack's greatest gift was to his listeners any time, most especially in baseball, where the daily broadcast means so much to so many, including the elderly, handicapped, and those who can't get to the ballpark. They would rise and fall with his exhilaration or

APIWWP

"Smith corks one into deep right field, down the line. It may go...Go crazy, folks! Go crazy! It's a home run, and the Cardinals have won the game 3-2, on a home run by the Wizard!"

— Jack Buck, October 14, 1985

"He had that booming voice, the voice. I used to tell guys, `You haven't made it to the big leagues until you've played the Cardinals and been on Jack Buck's show.'... When you heard the, 'Good evening, everybody, welcome to Cardinals baseball,' there was just something about that that sent chills down your spine."

— Ozzie Smith

AP/WWP

worry-wart fear of defeat. Many a night, like me—and I say for shame on both of us—he found sleep elusive after the bottom had dropped out for the home team, but he was a sensitive man.

With a throat golden until later illness, Buck used grammatical, glowing phraseology with knowledge and reserved detachment until he let it all hang out with, "Go crazy, folks, go crazy!" in his tribute to Ozzie Smith's first-ever left-handed home run that won a pivotal game in the 1985 League Championship Series. And, of course, the subtitle of his autobiography, "That's a Winner," sums up the man as well as his lingo and the life he led.

He had the precious gift defined by Mr. Webster as "mnemonics," the art of training or improving the memory. For those of us who think we can remember better, none can retain in memory better than this party of the first part who lived with third-person modesty. That great gift enabled him to think of a funny line and go to bed and remember it at lunchtime as a speaker.

Partly through mnemonics, Jack Buck was articulate with little effort because of that ability to retain what he had heard. He not only spoke Spanish well enough to warm the

Jack and Harry Caray at Stan Musial's induction into the Hall of Fame. According to Jack, "When Harry and I were doing the games together, we were as good a team as there ever was. His style and mine were so different that it made for a balanced broadcast. The way we approached the job, with the interest and love both of us had for the game, made our work kind of special."

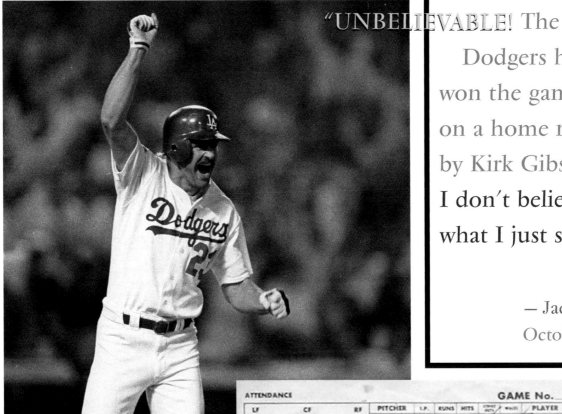

AP/WWP

"UNBELIEVABLE! The Dodgers have won the game on a home run by Kirk Gibson! I don't believe what I just saw!"

— Jack Buck,
October 1988

"I grew up with Ernie Harwell. Jack Buck is, like Ernie, an icon. Of course in 1988, when he made the call, it was a special attachment that lasted a lifetime. Let's say it was well said. I couldn't believe what I just saw, either."

— Kirk Gibson

homesick hearts of young tongue-tied Hispanics, but he also did well enough with German, French, and—ah, yes!—English.

With his time, talent and money linked with so many charities, Jack Buck was also just about the biggest tipper I ever saw. Not for ostentatious reasons, but because every buck Buck gave was a reminder of how tough it was to get one that matched his surname. He made many a day or night for a doorman, bellman, waiter, waitress, or any other service person he felt was underpaid or overlooked.

I was fascinated in death even more than in life with Jack's remarkable career. I was overwhelmed at how many people opened their hearts to him—physical visitations and souvenirs people brought, it was almost like he was a god. I was astonished and very impressed and very pleased that Jack had affected so many people.

"The thing that amazes me about [Jack]—and all of us have our own styles—he understated things to the extent that they more than adequately conveyed what people saw and thought. When Kirk Gibson hit the home run off Dennis Eckersley to win the World Series game, he said seven words: 'I don't believe what I just saw.' And that conveyed everything that people in Dodger Stadium were thinking [and] people watching on TV or listening on the radio. He said it exactly the way it was. That's a talent that very few people like us in this business have. He was amazing. He never big-timed anybody. He never thought he was important. He was genuinely amazed at the following he has. He was special; he really was."
—Hall of Fame Broadcaster
    Marty Brennaman

"INTO DEEP LEFT CENTER... and we'll see you tomorrow night."

— Jack Buck,
October 1991,
when Kirby Puckett
homered to send
the World Series to
Game 7.

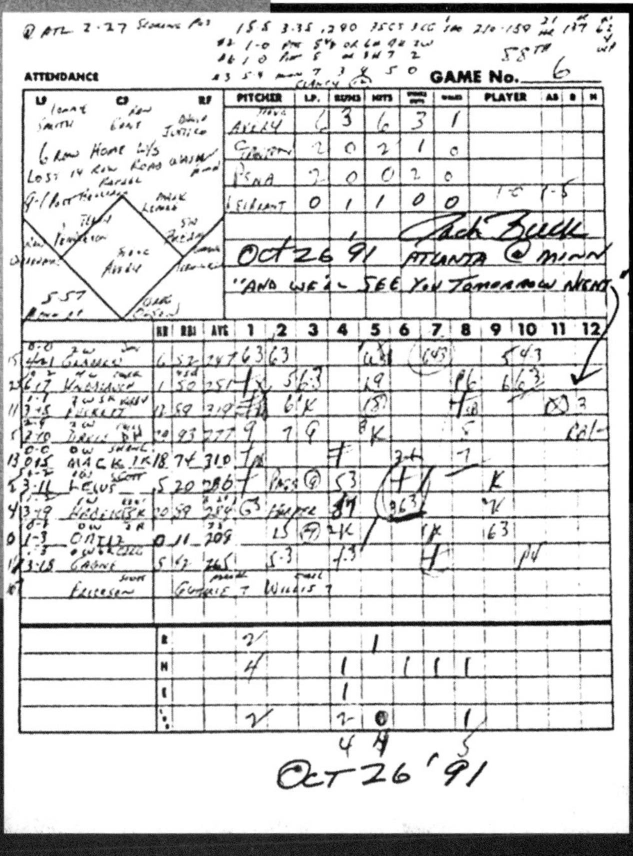

"Here's the pitch. Swing and there it goes. This is it. It's a home run.

Wake up, Babe Ruth, there's company coming

and it's Mark McGwire with home run number 60. They're going berserk here at Busch Stadium. Number 60 for McGwire. He couldn't have hit it higher. A historic moment here at Busch Stadium."
—Jack Buck, 1998

AP/WWP

"Bases empty for McGwire. Mike Morgan is the pitcher. Here it comes to McGwire. Swing—look at there, look at there, look at there. McGwire's number 61. McGwire's flight 61 headed to planet Maris. Home run McGwire. History. Bedlam. What a moment. He's shaking hands with the third basemen of the Cubs. **Pardon me while I stand up and applaud.** He picks up his son, Matt. He points to the fans. He points to the police officers on the field. Greeted by his teammates. What a Cardinal moment this is. What a baseball moment this is."
—Jack Buck, 1998

Mark

We expect the best to be better,
though we know it doesn't work that way.
There are inevitable limitations
that will always rule the day.

No matter what is accomplished,
a discovery, or a thought at the end of a pen,
it's, "What have you done for me lately?"
or, "Let's see you do that again."

In one glorious season
Mark McGwire turned the world upside down.
He blasted 70 homers.
The news whistled through every town.

The red-headed giant
was bold and defiant.
He was not to be thwarted that year.
He smashed the record by nine.
Lived in your life and mine
We took over his life, I fear.

McGwire has given his best,
never asked for a rest,
has recently spent time on the shelf.
Though they profess to respect him,
some still expect him
to constantly outdo himself.

But those who know him and love him
will always show him
admiration that need not be stated.
It was a remarkable year,
in a Hall of Fame career.
What great moments Mark McGwire has created.

It's Been

JFB

chapter
TEN

"I have the number-
one job in baseball.
Not the number-one
job in broadcasting,
but the number-one
job in baseball."

— Excerpt from Jack's
acceptance speech at the
Baseball Hall of Fame.

an Honor

Ford C. Frick Award
(National Baseball Hall of Fame)

"

Thank you, Ralph. And good afternoon ladies and gentlemen, Commissioner Ueberroth and folks of the baseball world. What a lovely day. What a great weekend and what a terrific honor. You'll be happy to know that I'm feeling fine and my pulse is at 169 and holding steady and I fully expect to get through this time period in good shape.

I was here twice previously, when Stan Musial was inducted, when Bob Gibson was inducted. And I had the pleasure of knowing the late Ford Frick. I shared a glorious moment with him one day in St. Louis, when Mr. Frick dedicated the statue of Stan "The Man" outside our Busch Stadium. And so because I knew Ford Frick, this award has even more meaning. So here stands a dirty-necked kid from Holyoke, Massachusetts wondering how in the heck he got here.

My eight kids are here. They're all boys except five. I wish they would stand, if I can remember their names. Beverly, Jack, Chris, Bonnie, Dan and Betsy down there in front. There's six of them. They're something. And I'd like to acknowledge their mother, Alyce. And down in front, Joe and Julie. And my wife Carole, who holds all of this together for me. I have a couple of brothers here, Earle and Frank. And another brother, Bob, and three sisters, Kathleen, Mary and Barbara.

I have the number-one job in baseball. Not the number-one job in broadcasting, but the number-one job in baseball. I don't want to be belligerent about it, but I kind of think, Mr. Steinbrenner and others, that St. Louis is not only the heartland of America, but the best baseball city in the United States. Boo me if you want, go ahead, that's what baseball's all about.

Ralph Kiner presents Jack with the Ford C. Frick award at the National Baseball Hall of Fame in Cooperstown in 1987.

This job transcends play-by-play. I have taken advantage of it to do some good things for Cystic Fibrosis, for the police department, Boys Town of Missouri, the Veterans Hospital, other hospitals, kids that need a helping hand, Mike Frey, Lance Holeshowser, and a kid back in St. Louis, who's as gutsy as a person as I ever met, John O'Leary. I've tried to help, I've tried to be a part of it.

I've had the pleasure of broadcasting Cardinal baseball. The first year I was there, '54, one Sunday afternoon in May, Stan Musial hit five home runs. I said, "My God, does he do this every Sunday?" He did *something* every Sunday. He didn't hit five home runs every Sunday. But imagine the people I've had the fun of describing: Boyer, McCarver and Maris, and Cepeda and Cunningham, and Javier and Groat, and currently Ozzie Smith and Jack Clark, and Willie McGee and Bob Forsch. And the best manager who ever managed, Whitey Herzog.

The biggest kick I get is to communicate with those exiled from the game, in hospitals, homes, prisons—those who have seldom seen a game, some who can't travel to the game, those who are blind. And after all of these years I realize that my energy comes from the people at the other end. The game has kept me young, involved, excited, and to be up here with the gems of baseball and this is like, for you people, I'm sure, looking at some diamonds in the front window of a jewelry store. For me to be standing up here is a thrill and a joy which I'll never forget.

> — Excerpts from Jack Buck's 1987 National Baseball
> Hall of Fame Ford C. Frick Award acceptance speech

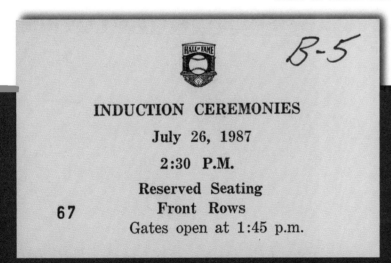

The Cardinals honored Jack on the field before a game after he returned home from his induction into Cooperstown. Jack then threw out the ceremonial first pitch.

I don't know exactly what it is

It's almost always been that way

No matter where I am, or who is there

I know exactly what to say

But there are times I draw a blank

and take on a certain air

Disinterested, or ill-equipped, I find I just don't care.

When I feel good, elevated, just right

and those around me don't

I should adjust, be as they are

I try to, I'd like to, but I won't

After all my years I've concluded

that those about me could be included

know my thoughts, my mood, my feelings

but to let them in would just be stealing.

So until there's nothing there

I'll exist with a particular air

It could have helped or just if they had known

But they, like I, are on their own.

Jack Buck
1995

RADIO
HALL OF FAME

"I'm grateful for the bat of Stan Musial, the arm of Bob Gibson, the legs of Lou Brock and the glove of Ozzie Smith. Turn the radio on, you'll hear a friend—you'll enjoy, you will learn, you will imagine, you will improve. Turn the radio on—at home, in your car, in prison, on the beach, in a nursing home—you will not be alone. You will not be lonely. Newspapers fold, magazines come and go, television self-destructs, [but] radio remains the trusted common denominator in this nation."

— Excerpt from Jack Buck's Radio Hall of Fame induction speech

Emmy Awards

At the Emmy Awards on April 26, 2000, Jack received the Sports Lifetime Achievement Award, and Joe took home the award for Outstanding Sports Personality Play-by-Play. Jack referred to Joe as "the Stan Musial of broadcasting—he combines a wonderful talent with a wonderful personality."

This year has been a year of change;
I've seen my life grow old.
My role has changed from boy to man.
My outlook must be bold.
Confidence must boil inside
My rather timid heart,
To prove to those who shake their heads
That I can play the part.

— poem written by Joe Buck at the beginning of
his broadcasting career

American Sportscasters Association Hall of Fame

"For a kid to end up in the Hall of Fame as a sports announcer after being a very poor athlete is astounding. I always played right field—batted 15th. The only time I played an entire game was when there was a flu epidemic in the neighborhood. When my father first saw me play baseball, he traded me for a son to be born later.

I really think I'm being inducted into the Hall of Fame because I was the only one that I know of who ever broadcast bowling on the radio."

— Jack Buck's remarks upon learning of his induction into the American Sportscasters Association Hall of Fame, 1990

chapter
ELEVEN

"Mr. Buck,
if I may borrow
your words,
pardon us while
we stand and
applaud."

— *Mike Matheny,
team spokesman at
Jack's memorial*

AP/WWP

"*So Long for*

Just a While

"Go crazy, heaven! Go crazy!"

Christine Buck

Christine's eulogy at her father's service, Twin Oaks Presbyterian Church, June 21, 2002.

"Nobody can prepare you for the death of a parent, regardless of the circumstances. The truth is we know we're lucky because so many people understand the depth of our loss. It's also their loss.

The phrase "random acts of kindness," I think, should have been invented for Dad. He understood something a lot of people *never* understand—the more you give, the more you get back—and he gave of himself in countless ways every day.

Our dad's philosophy was simple: It's either right or wrong, good or bad; you take this road or that road. He always said, "I like people. It's as simple as that. I like people to like me and I work at it." He had an incredible sense of humor. And it was just that, a sense—like hearing or smelling or touching. It was just who he was.

He was aging, but he never grew old. He was always charming and he could be disarming.

Once while golfing—a sport he loved that didn't always love him back—he looked at the caddie and said, "You are, without a doubt, the worst caddy I've ever seen." The caddie replied with a sly smile, "Oh no, Mr. Buck, that would be too big of a coincidence."

He was always in the moment, and not just when he was doing play-by-play. He was a fantastic master of ceremonies. He would prepare for a speaking engagement all the time. He always had scraps of paper sticking in his pockets. He said, "The cleaners know more about my business than I do."

"HEY, KID"

This photo of me and my Dad (opposite page) is one of my favorites. We were sitting outside holding hands when the photographer came around; we cuddled and the moment was captured. This night was especially memorable because it was his 75th birthday party and we were celebrating at my house. He was wearing his Cardinal red jacket, surrounded by family and friends. He loved every minute of that party! He always had a good time wherever he went and it was impossible not to have fun when you were around him. His love of life was contagious. He was a great man who is greatly missed by his family, friends and fans. I miss his phone calls, "Hey, kid. Listen to this poem," or "Hey, kid. Come on over. I've got some 'walking money' for you." I wish all my moments with my dad were captured in pictures like this one—feeling loved and safe in my father's arms.

-Christine
(a.k.a. Tina, but only by Dad)

Joe (left) stands with St. Louis Cardinals great Red Schoendienst as they watch a video tribute to Jack Buck, during the memorial ceremony at Busch Stadium.

AP/WWP

But you know, he never really *got* it. He never understood what he meant to this community. He used to say, "I'm a modest man with much to be modest about." We would beg to differ. He barely had a private persona. What you saw was what you got. He left a trail of love and laughter wherever he went.

Our father never walked; he strolled.

He raised the bar on a lot of things. Watching him struggle with his health and watching him struggle in the hospital, he raised the bar on what *we* can complain about.

He certainly raised the bar on tipping. We went to a car wash once and the manager dropped a hint to me and my sisters, "Your father tipped every guy in here $100 once." I looked around. There were 25 guys and I thought, "Sorry, buddy, I'm not my dad."

He raised the bar on being polite with good manners. He raised the bar on how to be classy and humorous and caring. He raised the bar on how to live life to its fullest. Don't waste time. Don't forget people less fortunate than you.

The love and support of this community has helped our family celebrate his life. And thank you for that. Thank you for understanding what a gem he was. The world is definitely a better place because of him.

We have to pick up the slack now; give more to charities; remember the veterans and people with cystic fibrosis and Parkinson's. If we all do random acts of kindness, we might be able to fill the void he left just a little bit.

On behalf of my family, "Thank you, St. Louis." We've said how we shared him, but the truth is, he wouldn't have it any other way.

"I will miss the style and elegance about him. I will miss the way people were drawn to him when he entered a room. I will miss that voice."

— Joe Buck

I want to read to you something that epitomizes what he means to his fans. This is from one of his fans—an anonymous letter that was left in front of his statue:

"Goodbye, old friend. It's time to say, 'Farewell.' You were always there in both good times and in bad. It seemed you always knew just what to say and most times you would say what I felt. You were my eyes when I could not see and my voice when I could not speak. You have lived the good life and fought the tough fight. It is now time for you to rest, old friend. We spent many years together and although we never met, you were a constant friend. On that I could depend. God has blessed your life and now it is time to be by His side. Go crazy, heaven! Go crazy!"

We love you, Dad, and we miss you. Goodbye. ■

— Christine Buck

"It was a great pleasure to know Jack Buck. It was always an uplifting experience to be in his company. His positive attitude, even in the face of his illness later in life, was a great example to all of us."

— *Stan Musial*

The Jack Buck Season

By Bonnie Buck

For most, the Super Bowl marked the end
Of the professional football season,
But for us and all who love you,
It just started—for this reason:

When we thought the game had ended,
It really just began.
What was supposed to be sudden death...
Went into overtime again.

Over and over and overtime again,
The coin that's flipped is getting thin,
But we're gonna end this game before
It's time for baseball to begin.

St. Louis lost the Super Bowl,
That was just their luck.
But then, with baseball 'round the corner,
It became the Season of Jack Buck.

A little hockey, some Olympic games,
The Final Four: Don't forget to bet!
Meanwhile, the Jack Buck Season keeps on goin'—
The game ain't over yet.

Overtime and overtime,
And still stuck in that bed,
But the quarterback has come up with a plan;
We'll end this game instead.

I can hardly wait for Tuesday;
Life will never be the same.
Because we'll be goin' crazy:
A "Hail, Mary" pass won the game.

Go crazy, folks.

"My voice of summer was silenced. After I wiped away a tear, I inserted my dusty Cardinals VCR tape and smiled as I listened to Jack Buck's gravelly voice describe Musial's corkscrew swing, Gibby's no-hitter, Brock's thievery and The Wizard's unlikely playoff homer. Mr. Buck was a boyhood fixture every steamy summer night on the old screened farmhouse porch in Cedar Hill, Missouri, a comforting voice amid the heat lightning, katydids and chiggers."

— *Jeff Welsch,*
Corvallis, Oregon
sports editor